Mayan Letters Charles Olson

Edited and
with a Preface by Robert Creeley

JONATHAN CAPE
THIRTY BEDFORD SQUARE
LONDON

First published in Great Britain 1968
by Jonathan Cape Ltd, 30 Bedford Square, London WCI
© 1953 by Charles Olson

SBN Paperback edition   224 61379 0
        Hardbound edition   224 61378 2

Condition of Sale

This book is sold subject to the condition that it
shall not, by way of trade or otherwise, be lent
re-sold, hired out, or otherwise circulated
without the publisher's prior consent in any form
of binding or cover other than that in which it is
published and without a similar condition being
imposed on the subsequent publisher.

Printed and bound in Great Britain
by Richard Clay (The Chaucer Press), Ltd
Bungay, Suffolk

CAPE EDITIONS 17

General Editor: NATHANIEL TARN

PREFACE TO THE FIRST EDITION

Some time towards the end of 1950, it was in December I think, but the letter isn't dated, I heard that Charles Olson was off to Yucatan. A sudden 'fluke' – the availability of some retirement money owed him from past work as a mail carrier – gave him enough for the trip, 'not much but a couple of hundred, sufficient, to go, GO be, THERE ... '. By February I had got another letter, 'have just this minute opened this machine in this house lerma ... ' From that time on I heard from him regularly, and so was witness to one of the most incisive experiences ever recorded. Obviously it is very simple to call it that, that is, what then happened, and what Olson made of his surroundings and himself. Otherwise, it is necessary to remember that Olson had already been moving in this direction, back to a point of origin which would be capable of extending 'history' in a new and more usable sense. In his book on Melville, *Call Me Ishmael*, he had made the statement, 'we are the last first people ... '; and in his poetry, most clearly in *The Kingfishers*, there was constant emphasis on the need to break with the too simple westernisms of a 'greek culture'.

Yucatan made the occasion present in a way that it had not been before. The alternative to a generalizing humanism was locked, quite literally, in the people immediately around him, and the conception, that there had been and *could* be a civilization anterior to that which he had come from, was no longer conjecture, it was fact. He wrote me, then, 'I have no doubt, say, that the American will more and more repossess himself of the Indian past ... If you and I see the old deal as dead (including Confucius, say), at the same time that we admit the new is of the making of our own lives & references, yet, there is bound to be a tremendous pick-up from history other than that which has been usable as reference, the moment either that history is restored (Sumer, or, more done, Chichen or Uaxactun) or rising people (these Indians, as campesinos ripe for Communist play – as ripe as were the Chinese, date 1921, June 30) ...' The problem was, to give form, again, to what the Maya had been – to restore the 'history' which they were. For in the Maya was the looked-for content: a *reality* which is 'wholly formal without loss of intimate spaces, with the ball still snarled, yet, with a light (and not stars) and a heat (not androgyne) which declares, the persistence of both organism *and* will (human) ...'

In editing the present selection, I have tried to maintain a continuity in spite of the limits of space and the loss of some letters which it has meant. I have indicated excisions with dots (...), whenever such were necessary.

ROBERT CREELEY

February 12th, 1953

Mayan Letters

saturday feb 18 (is it?)   lerma, campeche, mexico

Birds, lad: my god what birds. Last evening a thing
like our hawk. And that woman of mine (again) most
alert to their nature. It happened this way. I was down
the beach bargaining to buy a piece of their best fish
here, what sounds like madrigal, only it comes out
smedreegal. I had my back turned no more than three
minutes, when, turning, to come back to the house
(Con was on the terraza out over the sea, surrounded
by a dozen of these gabbling kids), below her, on the
water line, I noticed these huge wings fluttering
wrong. My guess was, one of the kids, all of whom
carry sling-shots, had brought down a zopalote (our
vulture, 'brother v,' as Con named them). But when I
came near, I noticed, just as Con cried down, that it
was no vulture but another bird which is quite beautiful here, in Maya a chii-mi (chee-me): flies in flock
over the waterline, soaring like hawks, high, and is
marked by a long splittail ((by god, i was right: just
checked dictionary, and is, as I thought, our frigate
bird))

there it was, poor chii-mi, stoned by one of
these little bastards, and the others, throwing more
stones at it, and a couple, kicking it. And it working
those three foot wings, hard, but not wild: very sure
of itself, tho downed. By the time I came up, it had

9

managed to get itself over, and was already out into the water, to get away from the kids. But each wave was wetting it down, and the misery was, that it drown.

My assumption was, the stone had broken its wing. But Con had seen it happen, and seems to have known it was only its head that had been struck (it was out cold, she told me later, for a minute or so, and then, on its back, had disgorged its last fish). Anyhow, she had the brains to send down one of the older boys to bring it out of the water, and up on the terraza. And when I came up, there it was, quiet, looking hard at everyone, with its gular pouch swollen like my Aunt Vandla's goiter, and its eye, not at all as a bird's is, when it is scared, or as, so quickly, they weaken, and that film drops over the eye. Not at all: this chii-mi was more like an animal, in its strength. Yet I still thought it was done for, something in the wings gone.

Just about then it started to work its way forward, pulling its wings in to its body, and making it look so much more like, say, a duck. What it had in mind, was to try to lift itself the two feet up to the wall that goes round the terraza. But it could not. It had worked itself into the inner angle of a corner. So I reached down and raised the right wing up to the top of the wall. Then the left. And, itself, it pulled its body up, perched for an instant, and swung off, off and up, into the sky, god help us, up and out over the sea, higher and higher, and, not like the others but working its wings in shorter, quicker strokes, it pulled off and off, out over the shrimp ship moored out in the deeper water, inside the bar, from which it swung inland again, and, as I watched it a good five minutes, kept turning more and more to the west, into the sun, until that peculiar movement of the wings began to give way to the more usual flight of a chii-mi. And I figure, as it disappeared, it was all right, all right.

God, it was wonderful, black, wonderful long feathers, and the wing spread, overall, what, five to six feet. Never got such a sense of a bird's strength, inside strength, as this one gave, like I say, more animal, seemingly, and sure, none of that small beating heart. That's why its victory, over these mean little pricks, was so fine.

(Its silhouette, anyway, above us each day, is a lovely thing, the fore part of the wing not a curve as in a gull, but angled like a bat's a third out from the body. And this strange double tail splitting in flight like the steepest sort of an arrow.

How come 'chii-mi' I can't yet tell you, though, last night, in my Dictionario Motul, which arrived yesterday from Merida and gives me a fair start in to the ride of this Maya tongue. I was able to locate 'chii,' as 'margin' of the sea, a page, a dress, etcetera. 'Mi' I still can't find in the proliferation of double consonants, double vowels, and five extra letters beyond Western alphabets (I daresay if I had Tozzer's Maya-English dictionary (the only one, I now learn), I'd be better off. To try to find anything through the screen of one unknown language to another! (this D. Motul is the base work, Maya-Espanol, done here in the Yucatan mid-16th century, and not equalled since. My edition is by the one Mexican scholar whom I have yet had occasion to raise respect for, a 82 yr old citizen named Juan Martínez Hernández.) ...

But I've been happier, by an act of circumvention, the last three days: I have been in the field, away from people, working around stones in the sun, putting my hands in to the dust and fragments and pieces of those Maya who used to live here down and along this road.

And the joy is, the whole area within the easiest walking distances, is covered with their leavings: I already have in front of me as I write to you the upper half of an owl idol's (?) head, which I picked up on a farm five minutes from the house! And two half plates, among other fragments of pots, quite fine in the working of the clay, though the painting is average.

The big thing, tho, is the solidity of the sense of their lives one can get right here in the fields and on the hill which rises quite steeply from the shore. Thursday afternoon Con and I went back in, say, five miles, and ran into something which would take the top off yr head: on the highest hill, looking out over a savannah which runs straight and flat to the sea here, a sort of farm moor (it was maize once, but, due to the way of Mayan agriculture, grass defeated corn inside of seven years, and from then on, the grass is so durable, neither forest nor corn can come again), on that hill

where the sea's winds reach, where the overlook is so
fine, these Maya had once built what appears to have
been a little city. I say appears, for now, after six
years of the Sanchez Construction Co. crushing the
stones of that city, we were able to see only one piece
of one column of what (the Indian workers told us)
was once, six years ago, many many such columns
in place! (The whole experience was like the deserts
we found in and around Sacramento, where the gold
Companies have, with their huge water shitting
machines, spoiled the earth (in this case not men's
work, but nature's soil accumulation, for ever, mind
you, forever: they turn the top soil down under and
pile on top of it, as their crawling machine goes along,
all the crunched gravel and stone their water-test has
proven not to contain gold, or the dust, of gold)

                                                    Crazy,
'stupido,' as the Indians at least, know it to be;
it angers me two ways (1) that the rubble
beneath the facings, columns, worked facades,
etc., is the bulk of the stone, and there is no reason
except laziness, that the worked things, so small a
part of the whole, should not have been set aside; and
(2) that this is the laziness, not of Sanchez & Co.,
which one has to grant its stupidity, but is the stupidity & laziness of the archaeologists, both American
& Mexican, which is that most culpable of all, intellectual carelessness.

              I had the feeling, already in
Merida, that the Peabody-Carnegie gang, whatever
they may have done, 50, or 25 years ago, were, now,

missing the job, were typical pedants or academics, and were playing some state & low professional game. Like this: that, at this date, it was no longer so important to uncover buried cities and restore same, as it was to strike in anew by two paths: (1) what I have already sounded off to you about, the living Maya language and what its perdurables, because language is so tough, may well contain in the heads of these living farmers back one block, from this street, or wherever, the deeper in, I imagine, the more and (2) in the present context the important one: a total reconnaissance of *all* sites (laugh as they did at me in Merida, the 'experts') instead of (as the Carnegie-Mexican Govt is about to launch) the recovery of the 3rd of the Maya Metropolises here in the peninsula, Mayapan.

The joker, is, they are 'advanced' enough to justify the Mayapan operation as a step to discover more abt the economic & political life of the ancient Maya! Which, of course, kills me. Here I am an aestheticist (which I have yet to be convinced *any* one of them, from Stephens on down, is). And now, when they, these professionals, are catching on (EP's 35 yr lag, surely), to the validity of the total life of a people as what cargo art discharges, I am the one who is arguing that the correct way to come to an estimate of that dense & total thing is not, again, to measure the walls of a huge city but to get down, before it is too late, on a flat thing called a map, as complete a survey as possible of all, all present ruins, small as most of them are.

They'll cry, these fat & supported characters: 'Oh, they are all over the place, these, ruins!' Which is quite, quite the big & astounding fact – so much so are they all over the place that Sanchez & Co., Campeche, Mex., is not the only sand & gravel company in business: already, in this walking area from this house, I have come to learn of four sites – and of some size more than 'small' – which have been already reduced to white cement in bags! That it has taken Sanchez six years of daily grinding at the site – no where, by the way, listed as a site – the natives here in Lerma call it Casa Vieja – to take only the face off the city, may be a gauge of ((what I had no way of knowing, in Merida)) the extent of these ignored, or smiled at, spots where, 1500 years ago, for 0, say, 500 years, a people went about human business …

2

monday feb 19 51 lerma

with a rice bowl full of the cheap rum here (35 cents by god, the qt), the kerosene lamp (my barn & hayrack), and yr long letter …

to start: (noting what you have noted that, the last two nights, the moon is coming to full) pick me up, thus –

by jeezus, if he didn't, having talked to me as much
as no common language permits – which is a very
great deal, given such a subject as, what a handsome
night it was, all these houses, and the rocks below this
white terraza. And the fucking night spreading itself
like a peee-cock, the birdless night, not a sound but
dogs, and the beginning of cocks, and the last of men
along the hill back off a bit. I, lying, like Cleo or some
olden knichte in stone, on the stone bed the wall of
the terraza makes, the head of the stair my fine pillow.
Having just thought, that fine white cayucos, would
make me a fine bed for the night, its sails, for some
reason, still in it, the masts, of course, shipped.

by jeezus if he didn't, having sd, bueno noche,
I, bonito, he, la luna, I, magnifico, he, presto – why,
I still don't know, whether, he was whistling so, –
and came from the direction of the cantina, down on
to the beach

anyhow, with, hasta manana, if he doesn't walk
straight out into the water to that magical boat, swing
himself aboard, take up his bow line, haul himself
off, by the stern line, a few twenty feet (enough to
take care of the fall of the tide), heave off a heavier
grab-iron, start moving around fixing the sails to his
liking, light himself a cigarette, and lie right down
there to sleep!

jee-zus – it's handsome. I am like a kid. Tonight, I
swear, I never saw Venus lay down a path of light on

water. She does. Has set, now. Stars: please make me
a map of the handsomer constellations (I know Orion,
the two dippers (stupid names). But what is that string
of seven, or is it eight, which run down the sky to the
west of Castor & Pollux? ((All I see is the movement
of the west sky, we front the west so decisively. And
the house blocks off, the other half. But enough, what
is, to make me wild, wild (not like beautiful Lawrence,
 don't mean, who, fr the full of the moon, is sd, to
have got like the throat of his fringed gentians) but
wild as I am which is not wild but cool, real cool

God, give me a little more of this and I shall
excuse what you say abt me, another time, my friend.
For you have said something so beautifully tonight,
in this business of force: it is (you see, I am still harp-
ing on this problem of mine, reference: constellations,
Venus included (which, here, I will show can be called
KuKulCan – abandoned such, as part of THE K's and
THE PRAISES, discovering this man's death, April 5,
1208 AD, who 'rose' with Venus, 8 days later, was
sufficient unto itself, so far as I was concerned) what
you sd: that, force STAYS, IS & THEREFORE STAYS
whenever, whatever:

that is what
we are concerned with
It breaks all time, & space.
muy bueno, muy

BONITO

3

tues. (carlos, the letter carrier, abt due / sort of th
village idiot, i take it : walks like no fisherman
smiles like a gringo, and is altogether nc
native, is 'allegre,' slap-happy, and of whom
am most fond : yesterday, bringing yr letter, h
holds out two us air mail sts (enclosed)! I say
how come, and, as I understood, he had noticec
that, they had not been cancelled. So he ha
carefully removed them from the envelopes
and brought them to me! So here they are, fo
you.

You will imagine, knowing my bias to
ward just such close use of things, how much
all these people make sense to me (coca-cola
tops are the boys' tiddley-winks; the valves c
bicycle tubes, are toy guns; bottles are used ant
re-used, even sold, as cans are; old tires are th
base foot-wear of this whole peninsula (th
modern Maya sandal is, rope plus Goodyear)
light is candle or kerosene, and one light to a
house, even when it is a foco, for electricidad

and last night, at the store, for a beer, afte
they had closed, got into one of those conver
sations one does, with storekeepers, when they
are sloping off: the wife was pinching off &

peppercorns per packet of newspaper (5 cen-
tavos) / the page was open to a television ad
(Mexico City) / they both ask me / I say MALO,
MAS MALO QUE RADIO / but then, sez the
husband, the straight and surest question im-
aginable (Newsreel Companies please note, as
well as the Dept of Disappearing Culture) –
POSSIBLE TO SEE LA GUERRA?

by god, that kills me: Con tells me a kid on
the beach went straight to the same, 1st question, too : possi-ble, to see, la GUERRA? ...

4

Sat. Feb 24   (51)

... Have moved ahead some on what I suppose I am
here for. And one badly damaged fresco at Chichen
is a good part of cause, joined to what I have been
able to figure, from the number of ruins right back of
me, & Martínez, my good fisherman who becomes
the live object to spark it all. Figure – just to keep
cutting in – to go along on this notion: that none of
the characters have spotted two things (rather, they
have suppressed one, and been blinded, by maize, to
the other):

(1) that the sea, precisely the FISH, was of first imagi-
    native importance to the Maya (as well, of course,

19

crucial to his food economy: I just might add a
correlative to Sauer's beautiful shot, about maize
– he made clear to the boys that the very place
where starch crops can be domesticated (moderate
plateaus), where maize was (the inland slopes of
the cordilleras, Guatemala) cuts the people off from
the most abundant source of protein and fat there
is, the sea, that the earliest American farmers were
just so cut off

based on Lerma, plus some pots I have
been looking over from the island of Jaina up the
coast a distance, here, plus the paintings at Chi
chen, I take it I could, if I wanted to, demonstrate
that the movement into the Yucatan peninsula
might just have been a push for protein & fat,
(contradicting the mystery abt same that all of
these half-heads of great name keeping pushing
along to perpetuate their profession)

the real proof may turn out to be one of those
lovely curves of live human connections. I must
have sketched this bird Stromsvik, whom Con and
I got drunk with, in Merida? Well, in the midst of
his beer, Gus says, in Campeche, one guy, Hippo
lito Sánchez. The 1st day we walk into the museum
here, we pick up, and take for a beer, this Sánchez
(who is worrying a white puppy, with a red ribbon
that he was due to take to his girl friend, which
taking I delayed a good hour, which lad Sánchez
proving himself, did the delay well by (how many
do you know who can take that kind of pressing?)

So this week, I saw, why, Gus, had, what had caused Gus to say, Sánchez (in fact the very same stuff which had led Gus to get this kid assigned to go to Bonampak to aid the 'artists' sent there to take off copies of these newest discovered of all Mayan frescoes) : huge drawings hundreds of them, of the GLYPHS on the stairway of the major pyramid at Copan (Honduras)

my god, those you must see, some day : I am already taking steps to see if there is not some way to get them published. It is the only time I have found the drawings of glyphs to begin to touch the registration of the stone itself (and let me tell you the stones themselves are one hell of a job to see)

this boy has the hand, eye, heart, to get them over. And by god, if right spang in the middle of looking over his pages do I see the most certain demonstration of the power of the fish over these peoples I have yet oc

      Goddamn son of a bitch, if the 'f' in the machine didn't just go & bust – fuck it. Will have to go Campeche, & hope to christ a fix possible.

Well, to hell with fish – I obviously can't say much more about them, today, without the 'f' on this fucking machine.

One other thing, tho, while it's in my head, that I wanted to say to you: don't let even Lawrence fool you (there is nothing in this Mexican deal, so far as 'time in the sun' goes: the way I figure it, it must have seemed attractive at a time when the discouragement, that the machine world goes on forever, was at its height

but this is a culture in arrestment, which is no culture at all (to this moment, only Sánchez gives a hint of live taste)

when I say that, however, I give these people much more head, than their recent slobberers

for the arrestment, surely, was due to the stunning (by the Spanish) of the Indian, 400 yrs ago ((the Indian has had the toughest culture colonialism to buck of anyone, much tougher than that which Parkman & Melville beat, 100 yrs ago, up there culture

is confidence, & surely, Mao makes Mexico certain, ahead (Communism, here, by the way, is solid, but is, as not in the States, nor, so far as I have been able to judge, in Russia or Europe either, a cultural revolution, or at least the weapon of same, the only one the Indian (like the Chinese?) has been able to get his hands on (this whole Peninsula – where Cardenas got his familiar name: 'The Old Man,' in Mayan – is a muzzle rammed for firing)

The point is, the arrestment, is deceptive: it is not what fancy outsiders have seen it as, seeking, as they were, I guess, some alternative for themselves (like DHL & his Ladybird). Of course, now, it is easier to kiss off the States, than, even the 30's. Yet, they should not have misled us (which is the same as harming these Injuns: they have so fucking much future, & no present, no present at all. (Christ, it makes me burn: their inactivity ain't at all beautiful. They are fucking unhappy. What graces they have are traces only, of what was & of what, I'd guess, can be (to be a colored people today is something! Yah?

But the Negro in the States is way ahead of these 400 yr slept people! Sounds crazy? Hell, straight: yr Hyderabad drums, for ex: jesus, the only thing you have here, any place, when they make music (which is little) is the drum. But stacked up against Baby Dodds or whoever, pigeon shit – or what is most important, stacked up against these old Mayan drums I've worked out on – five, so far, cut out of trees – you should hear them.

And the sounds they put into the feet & bottoms of their pots, those people, to make noises, when you placed them, or moved them, on the table! ...

Point (2) above, was VIOLENCE – killing, the heart, out, etc: those sons of bitches, those 'scholars' – how they've cut that story out, to make the Mayan palatable to their fucking selves, foundations, & tourists!

lerma   march 8

Yr letter! How it spotted itself. This way: (1) arrived
precise to eclipse of sun (½); (2) arrived at climax of
long gab with Con in which ... I had made this proposition: that Kukulkan vs the Chichimec was the
true contest, not the Spanish, and that I proposed to
pick up again, now here, on the life of this very great
man, saying to Con, that, with so much registration
of him in codices, frescoes, stone cutting, stucco, it
should be as possible, or more, to recreate him as, that
Barlow, from mss., sought to do same by Montezuma:
                                                                had
just sd, 'I forgot to tell you, that, at Champoton,
after you took the bus last Sunday, I got into conversation with a bar boy, there, and, talking abt the
Isla Cuyo (the remnant now standing in the sea
of the pyramid K had erected for himself, there,
on departing Tula-ward, he having done his work,
here), it was my notion, that, that he had the
imagination to build *in the sea*, was another sign of
how unique he was' (asking myself, the relation of
same act to (1) the fact that the Maya hereabouts put
their cities (in contrast to all since) on the hill over
the sea ('Señor gusta monte,' sd the lady, fr whom,
bananas, on the road in, one day), (2) the Island of
Jaina, just above us here, abt as far north of us as

Champoton is south, and not yet visited because it *has* to be *reached by sea* (had most beautiful workmen in clay), and (3) that, on the east coast, the big beautiful place is TULUM, and, the *Island* of Cozumel (by map in yesterday fr Tulane, the sites on Cozumel are thick ((propose to go there, if possible to swing it: three days by sailing vessel from Progreso))

when LETTER-LIGHT, comes in the midst of a context unduplicatable – (1) the stir outside with all, *all*, kids & grown ups, watching, the eclipsa, excited (contrast to States, abt 1930, when, a total eclipse, and only me and the birds, apparently, aware, until it was suddenly dark) here, with no real shrinkage of light, yet, everyone, these descendants of astronomers, than whom none more effective than one Kukulkan, apparently ((the month CEH, as, I believe, in last letter I identified as HIS new fire ceremony – Spinden dates its institution as 1168 with a Day 1 Knife, when K started a year count as Year 1 Knife, and in Year 2 Reed, 1194–5, he declared the Fire Ceremony to be celebrated at intervals of 52 years)) all of them, with smoked glass and old film and rolled up newspapers, anything, looking, upward; (2) the conversation, me still beating around, these things

&

(3) CARLOS WALKS IN WITH YR NEWS, YR NEWS, BRO, OF K & a sea-horse (for same thing, a sea-horse, is also precise: using as fetish to hold down yr letters in the wind which sweeps through this room, what

do I have, have had since third day after arrival, as present from a boy I have never seen since? and same thing I have thought again & again, it's light, and I should like to send it to you & Ann & kids as SIGN, but haven't because, to box something seems beyond huge, for to get a letter off, a money order say, is already proved murder: one for book fr Merida lost already!

And now it is too late. For you have it, already. And have made me the present! Beautiful. And tell Slater, for me, he's HOT. Or so I'd guess, round abt now, with, what is in hand:

Let me go back.

I: why I still beat up against this biz of, getting rid of nomination, so that historical material is free for forms now, is

Ez's epic solves problem by his ego: his single emotion breaks all down to his equals or inferiors (so far as I can see only two, possibly, are admitted, by him, to be his betters – Confucius, & Dante. Which assumption, that there are intelligent men whom he can outtalk, is beautiful because it destroys historical time, and

thus creates the methodology of the Cantos, viz, a space-field where, by inversion, though the material is all time material, he has driven through it

so sharply by the beak of his ego, that, he has
turned time into what we must now have, space
& its live air

((secondary contrast is Joyce, who, it comes to
me now, did not improve on Duns Scotus Eri-
genus, or the Irish of the time the Irish were the
culture-bosses, what was it, 7th–9th century, or
something: he tried to get at the problem by
running one language into another so as to
create a universal language of the unconscious.
Which is, finally, mush & shit, that is, now. Not
so, then, DSE or Irishers, for then Europe was,
both in language & dream, of that order.

(((further thot: Joyce, the Commercial Tra-
veller: the worship of IARichards – by the
same people, accurately enough, who mug
Joyce – is more honest: that is, that this
internationalizing of language is more rele-
vant to commerce, now, than it is to the
aesthetic problem.
((((all this a bet-
ter way to say, he, ENDER)

the primary contrast, for our purposes is, BILL:
his Pat is exact opposite of Ez's, that is, Bill HAS
an emotional system which is capable of exten-
sions & comprehensions the ego-system (the Old
Deal, Ez as Cento Man, here dates) is not. Yet

by making his substance historical of one city (the Joyce deal), Bill completely licks himself, lets time roll him under as Ez does not, and thus, so far as what is the more important, methodology, contributes nothing, in fact, delays, deters, and hampers, by not having busted through the very problem which Ez has so brilliantly faced, & beat

Which ought to – if my mouth had words in it, this morning – bring you to see why I hammer, on, nomination, thus:

each of the above jobs are HALVES, that is, I take it (1) that the EGO AS BEAK is bent and busted but   (2) whatever it is that we can call its replacement (Bill very much a little of it) HAS, SO FAR, not been able to bring any time so abreast of us that we are in this present air, going straight out, of our selves, into it

You see, I followed you, a bit back, when, in responding on Tarot & Maya, you sd, sure, & it's whatever you or anyone makes hot, is hot. Of course.

& two: that, we already have both (1) the ego as responsible to more than itself and (2) absolute clarity, that, time, is done, as effect of work in hand

Perhaps, as I sd before, I am only arguing with myself, that is, I am trying to see how to throw the materials I am interested in so that they take, with all impact

of a correct methodology AND WITH THE ALTER-
NATIVE TO THE EGO-POSITION

I keep thinking, it comes to this: culture displacing
the state. Which is my guess as to why Ez sounds so
flat, when, he is just talking, when, he is outside the
Cantos, say, that walker of his, than which there is,
yet, no better
    (so much of Ez is, the 19th-century stance:
    PROTEST, (Dahlberg is the funny man, of same
            biz: they both wld love to have been,
            who was it, Lousie 14th, 'l'état, c'est
            moi'?
            what burns me, is, they never speak, in
            their slash at the State or the Economy,
            basically, for anyone but themselves.
            And thus, it is Bohemianism

            and much too late, just abt as late as be-
            fore Fourier, Marx, & Nietzsche, not to
            mention the real guys, then, Riemann
            or any of the geometers who were really
            cutting ahead

    Tho, again, here, one has to give Ez his due: that
    he did write KULCH

Which ought to get us to II, or, Kulkulkan. This
way:
          why the problem is tougher than Ez's throw,
or Bill's failure, is that, the shift is SUBSTANTIVE (it

delights me, to recognize, that, the word has that other meaning, of 'noun'!)

that is, another reason why i don't think Ez's toucan works after 1917 is, that, after that date, the materials of history which he has found useful are not at all of use (nor are Bill's, despite the more apparent homogeneity: date 1917, not only did Yurrup (West, Cento, Renaissance) go, but such blueberry America as Bill presents (Jersey dump-smoke covering same) also WENT (that is, Bill, with all respect, don't know fr nothing abt what a city *is*)

the which says this: that the substances of history now useful lie outside, under, right here, anywhere but in the direct continuum of society as we have had it (of the State, same, of the Economy, same, of the Politicks: Ez is traitor as Dante was, to Florence: the difference of F to USA is not difference at all, other than, the passage of time & time's dreary accumulations by repetition

(((something of this must have been what Razl meant, when he sd, HISTORY IS UNIVERSAL MONOTONY)))

(*Note*: I note that I assume history is prime, even now. I assume it is. I assume this one thing – man's curiosity abt what his brother zopalotes have been about – comes through to us straight from that previous civilization,

and is the one thread we better damn well
hang on to. And the only one.

Perhaps because it is as much prime, as, an
eclipse?

The substance has changed. Period. BUT: we are confronted, as men forever are, by the LAG. Our fellow
cits are, I take it, quite easily thrown off by any noun
which contains Z's and X's. (Not, again, that, thus
superficially, it matters a good god damn: bust them
over the heads. Right. Only, what i am saying is, that,
to use X's and Z's makes for the difficulties
John Adams, or King Fu Sze, or even Omeros,
don't. ((Or is this just a little bit argumentative, & pet-
    ulant, as one is, when the work is not done,
    and one is talking abt it instead.))
        ((Doesn't matter. For, as you'd guess, the
        operation is otherwise, is, actually, the
        other edge: how *was* this Kukulkan, how
        are you, Mister C)))

How can I pick up these injuns – that is, as Stephens,
Prescott, Parkman did not so pick them up 100 yr
agone, that, at the same moment of time as one H.
Melville, they made them stick as he did, Pacifica?
What's wrong – or, likewise, Sumeria. Or mao. Or
usa, today.

NO. Erase the above. Somewhere I've been dragged
off the methodological, here, by my own mention of

the substantive. And am sucked into a substantive argument. Which is not what we're here for. Let me try it another way. For it's still this man Kukulkan we are talking abt.

Shots:

(1) are not the Maya the most important characters in the whole panorama (diorama was the word contemporary to above fine 4 workers) simply because the TOP CLASS in their society, the bosses, were a class whose daily business was KNOWLEDGE & its OFF-SHOOT, culture?

that thus a man of K's temper & interest could become Big Boss, & then, God?

and that any such society goes down easily before a gun? or bows & arrows, when Chichemecs come along with same? ((The absolute quote here, is, one prime devil, Goebbels, who sd: 'When I hear the word "kultur" I reach for my gun.'))

(2) that such a society is precisely the contrary (really the contrary, not the opposite, to use Blake's careful discrimination, and, by so doing, show up the collective or communist deal for what it is, and will continue to be as long as the rest of the world wants what America has had

Comes up, out out of the sea, a sea
horse (my question is, where
here
do the rains
come from, is the serpent
who shall fight the jaguar
another norther, of
another season, is
weather, here, as on the earth because
the earth turns eastward, is
all movements, as was the people's coming, is it from
the west?
they say
he was the wind, they say
also rain, anyway
he was water, not
sun fire not this heat which makes the day less
than the night

he wore a hat, a sort of silly hat, had
short breeches, a tortoise back with mirror on it, and
a tail: he died
just as the heat was at its worst, just
on the day the fields were burnt, just that day the
    morning
star rose anew
            his eyes, she sd,
            were like a caracol. And when he left us, he
            walked straight out into the sea, west
                        he was also
                        a bachelor

seemed most important, he
was just, was
a child
of water, they figured it, was
precisely what
they needed, was
the image of
(Well! To hell with that. Pardon me. Get up off my
face, olson.)
themselves.

It is a beautiful thing, what Slater found. You are
right, of course: it bears right in on what I have
been turning over. I figure, now, that why (as I
think I told you) I abandoned him in the two throws
of The K's and The P's, was, that, it is this thing, of
the sea, which one finds out here. And nobody told
me. And which sea is the addition to him as Venus,
which, makes up a package.

A favor: if you have an encyclopedia at hand, or any
source, could you write me what this damned star
Venus does with itself in a year? That is, is there a
coincidence of its brightest brightness with April 12th
or thereabouts? We await, e.g., that day, or c., because, they tell us, on that date the farmers burn their
fields, and, for a month, it is here as tho there were
an eclipse – or as it was, there, last fall, when the
Canadian woods were burning down   FORGET IT.
I guess the time has come for me to dig this biz. And

it's large. And better be done whole (all I was after I'll tell you another day. But 1st:

What cools me, is a sentence like this fr Spinden:

'Date I: 11- 8-14- 3-16, 10 Cib 4 Yax, May 5, 1136

This phenomenon took place before the Toltecs had conquered Chichen Itza but easily enough it may represent data upon which Quetzalcoatl worked and which possibly he presented in his Sacred Book.'

or

'In the Vienna Codex the Venus staff' which Quetz is chief bearer of 'is stuck in a valley between two hills beside a trumpet shell' (which trumpet shell Con & I find plenty of – even found one at K's Isla – and is, of course, our sea-shell, or, here, the CARACOL (the astronomers' house at Chichen is, a snail!)

It's the damndest thing, what a cat I got by the tail. For, you see, here is this supposed land-maize people who use
(1) for the house which brought them culture, the astronomy house, a SEA-SHELL
(2) for the man who appears to have made the language of this people for time in the universe available to all neighboring peoples, a SEA-HORSE!

And – this had broke in on me before I got yr letter
with Slater's shot, yesterday – THE EVIDENCES
Spinden here above is referring to, are not Maya. but
MIXTEC, in other words, of the Central Valley of
Mexico, not Yucatan. SO THAT, the whole picture
has shifted wider & out, west: in fact, what i ought
to be, am, proposing, is, THE SEA IN MAYA &
MEXICAN CULTURES & ECONOMIES.

AND   AND,
somewhere in this mixing of the two geographies is
the key to why there is a KUKULKAN here, &
QUETZ there: same man, same imagery (the serpent
with fuzz) (SEA-SERPENT?)

What the astronomy establishes, is, that the complex is WATER: that is, Venus-sign (Q & K Venus-
God, April 13, 1208 thereafter) is "Nine WIND." Is
also RAIN (the seasonal need). Is also; somehow,
SERPENT (contrary of sun, which is, Jaguar). Is –
shall we allow, for the present – SEA-H. In other
words, see what I mean: snails, for noise, water, for
maize, and a man, fr the west, where (does it) the
wind (yes, northers) & the rain (also?) come from ...

(O, yes, as of the wind: the drawing of K or Q most
like ann's s .. h ...., is, actually, not of him himself
but of the wind, God K of the Codices, who is, to be
sure, by reasoning from a like union in Mexican
mythology, seen as K:

let me send back that drawing, for, Ann's
to me:

6

sat march 17

christamiexcited. getting that load off my heart, to
you, thursday, did a trick. for i pulled out, that afternoon, down the road AND BROKE THRU–

> hit a real spot, which had spotted fr bus,
> and which same, apparently, untouched:
> Con & I came back with bags of sherds
> & little heads & feet – all lovely things

> then, yesterday, alone, hit further south,
> and smash, dug out my 1st hieroglyphic
> stone! plus two possible stela (tho, no
> crowbar, so no proof)

> and today I went to hit again, while the
> run's on : and the joy that everything I can
> get to, in an hour (necessary, however,
> to risk getting a ride back, bumming:

last night, took until 10:30, with Con, here, sure, fr a conversation of warning fr a friend the night before, scaring the shit out of both of us, that snakes will get you! she saw me in the wilds with no one to suck the wound, and this morning, the zopalotes eating me, with the rising sun!) To tell the truth, I was scared, yesterday, where I was, for the 1st half hour. Then, the excitement, the loveliness, the hell with it ...

Had started to reply ... But my nerves are so bunched toward these ruins, I better go and get back to these things later, if you will understand, please. For I am wild for it.

Example: the big baby I spotted yesterday means CHUNCAN means TRUNK OF THE SKY – and by god, the pyramid is so sharp and high it is just that, and most beautiful, high over the sea and the land (more like a watch-tower than anything templish ...

7

tuesday, march 20

... picking up, going back, over: (1) Ann, was shooting good, on the agronomy ... only it's a little different, and, another measure of – a damn good mea-

sure of – what machines, in their laziness, lead to:
viz – unlike India, the soil, here, is most shallow, a
few inches, & only occasionally, in drift pockets, 6
inches or more. So the struggle of the roots is intense.
But a long time ago the boys beat it this way. It's
grass that is the big enemy of maize, the only real
one, for they burn off the bush, before they plant.
But grass keeps coming in. And in the old days, they
were able to stand it off – for as long as seven years
(the maximum life of a milpa) – by weeding out the
grass by *hand*. But then came the machete. And with
it, the victory of grass in *two* years. For ever since
that iron, the natives cut the grass, and thus, without
having thought about it, spread the weed-seed, so that
the whole milpa is choked, quickly choked, and gone,
forever, for use for, maize (grass is so tough it doesn't
even let bush or forest grow again!)

One curious corollary, that, the Communist future of
this peninsula will have to reackon with: that, the
ground is such, and its topography so humped &
rocked, that, still, the ancient method of planting –
with a pointed stick, and sowing, with the hands –
is far superior to any tractor or planter or whatever.

So I wonder very much about Slater's pass,
that the Maya were far too intelligent a race to ex-
haust their soil, not to speak, as you are right to
question, of his observation, that they were a highly
spiritual race and such races always regard their soil
as sacred :

for example, what i can't find anything out about, is WATER. Judging from the bizness here now – and adding it to the *apparent* fact that the Maya depended, for water, upon these accidents of nature, where the upper limestone crust collapsed, and created these huge cenotes, near which they built their cities – I'd guess that this people had a very ancient way of *not improving on nature*, that is, that it is not a question of either intelligence or spirituality, but another thing, something Americans have a hard time getting their minds around, a form or bias of attention which does not include *improvements*

AND (by that law of the toilet, beds, etc., I wrote you about once, from Washington – how I can never worry) I'm not one myself to say they were *backward*, *are* backward (my god, talk about the stars here: I ought to get off to you about the *flesh* here! Jesus, to ride a bus with these people, of a Sunday, down the coast, the stopping, the variation of quality between, say, Seybaplaya (allegre) and La Jolla (a sugar cane plant there, and a bottom, all, creatures, most of them, garage proletariat – to steal, an accurate, phrase)

BUT, the way the bulk of them still (the 'unimproved') wear their flesh! It is something I never had the occasion to guess, except in small pieces, isolated moments like, say, an Eyetalian family, or some splinter, not making itself clear enough to take over my assurances. For this is very much the result, I'd take it, as, the agriculture, the water problem: the flesh is worn as

40

a daily thing, like the sun, is – & only in this sense – a common, carried as the other things are, for use. And not at all exclusively sexual, as, it strikes me, the flesh is hardened, and like wires, focused ('foco' is the name for an electric light bulb, here) in the industrial States. The result (and this is what I think is actually the way to put what Slater makes spiritual or sacred) is, that the individual peering out from that flesh is precisely himself, is, a curious wandering animal (it is so very beautiful, how animal the eyes are, when the flesh is not worn so close it chokes, how human and individuated the look comes out: jeesus, when you are rocked, by the roads, against any of them – kids, women, men – it's so very gentle, so granted, the feel, of touch – none of that pull, away, which, in the States caused me, for so many years, the deepest sort of questions about my own structure, the complex of my own organism, I felt so very much this admission these people now give me

This is not easy to state, I guess. BUT OF EXTREME IMPORTANCE. For I come on, here, what seems to me the real, live clue to the results of what I keep gabbing about, *another* humanism. For it is so much a matter of resistance – like I tried to say, about, *leaving* the difficulties, not removing them, by *buying* the improvements so readily available at the corner. You buy something all right, but what gets forgotten is, that you sell, in that moment of buying – you sell a whole disposition of self which very soon plunders you just where you are not looking. Or so, it seems.

The
trouble is, with this imagery, of industrial man.
I distrust it, as (1) too easy (2) too modern and (3)
too much, not contrary, but merely oppositional.
For the shift, which took away, (is taking away,
so rapidly, that I shall soon not be able to get into
Campeche, it is such an ugly ('feo,' is their word)
demonstration of what happens when COMMERCE
comes in) – how do you get at what happened?
when did some contrary principle of man get in business? why? what urge

well, that's not hard, I know – i figure it always was,
only, once (or still, here, at Seybaplaya – and a bit
back, Lerma, before electricity) these big-eared, small-
eyed, scared-flesh characters stayed as the minority,
were not let out of, their holes. Because there was a
concept at work, not surely 'sacred,' just a disposition
to keep the attention poised in such a way that there
was time to (1) be interested in expression & gesture
of all creatures including at least three large planets
enough to create a system of record which we now
call hieroglyphs; (2) to mass stone with sufficient proportion to decorate a near hill and turn it into a fire-
tower, or an observatory, or as one post of an
enclosure in which people, favored by its shadows,
might swap camotes for shoes; (3) to fire clay, not just
to sift and thus make cool water, or, to stew iguana,
or fish, but to fire it so that its handsomeness put
ceremony where it also belongs, in the most elemen-

tary human acts. And when a people are so disposed, it should come as no surprise that, long before any of these accomplishments, the same people did an improvement, if one likes, of nature – the domestication of maize – which is still talked of as one of the world's wonders!

It is all such a delicate juggling of weights, this culture business – exactly like, I'd guess, what is the juggling of any one of us with the given insides. Which is why generalization is, a greased slide.

Christ, these hieroglyphs. Here is the most abstract and formal deal of all the things this people dealt out – and yet, to my taste, it is precisely as intimate as verse is. Is, in fact, verse. Is their verse. And comes into existence, obeys the same laws that, the coming into existence, the persisting of verse, does.
                                                                    Which
leads me to use again Ruth Benedict's excellent proposition (to counter the notion that, the Maya, having done so much, need also have developed an agronomy which would not have exhausted their soil and a system of rain-gathering which would also have licked the thirst problem) : says Benedict,

   ... techniques of cultural change which are limited
   only by the *unimaginativeness of the human mind*

Or which, perhaps, is just a little bit the bitterness of an old-maid almost-Communist before she died. It seems to me now, she over-loads, by using 'imagination,' even negatively – a little bit too much modern

Hamletism (I am thinking of Hamlet to Horatio (is it) on what a glory man is, the top creature, what nature, was working toward, etc.) Benedict is still the reverse of same. One needs to be quieter – but still not miss the point: that, in a given lifetime a man, or, in a given expression, a culture cannot get any more done than it can get done: that time, & our life-machine, are not infinitely extensible. Which dream – the Renaissance, & all ecstatic propositions – is well dead. We'll know more and do more if the limits – there'll be more reaches, etc.

My point is, what more do we have the privilege to ask of the Maya than same Maya offered ...
CHUN-CAN, by the way, which I told you was TRUNK OF THE SKY, is – says Martínez – not that (which is what the Seybanos told me) but TRUNK OF THE SERPENT. He says, to be the 1st, it would have to be CHUN-CAAN. (Which of course it may have been.)

8

Lerma   March 22 51

It is Holy Week in this Spanish nation, so I imagine the reason we have not had any mail since the week-end is, that the airplanes are blessing themselves, and doing other services over the middle of the Gulf. It irritates me, as do all Sundays, holidays and such:

tho yesterday, I shall say it was pleasant, sitting in a Coney Island stand (the best cafe Campeche can offer, on a sidewalk – or, for Vera Cruz, on such a day), eating turkey tacos, & drinking mineral water! (We had had to go in, at 10 A.M. to settle an argument over the rent of this house – which we lost, I am afraid: the two owners got into a snarl a month ago, and I was hoping we could take advantage of it to force the rent back to what we expected to pay when we came. But I guess not: it was fun, trying – and much worth while, for 5 bucks difference, here, is a good week's food.

In any case, the whole uproar brings on the problems of what I ought to do, running out, as I am, so fast, of funds. It burns my arse, to be put to it – and just when I begin to pick up, feel freshened, toughened, and hoisted forward. It is that old problem, how a man, whose goods are not bought, whose daily drive turns out to be non-economic (Corman tells me we are all dollar-an-issue men) eats, sleeps, gets on, with his work.

I keep turning over, where to strike out, for a stake … The only hitch is, the extremity fast approaches, god damn it. Which interrupts my mind. And deters, deters!!

But not much. Have been digging the old Maya chronicles, the last couple of days, and come up with interesting stuff on Quetz-Kukul – and the question of,

45

sea origins. Will be folding it yr-way, I suspect, soon. One curious thing is, that the place of origin (in the legends) keeps coming up as TULE (also Tula, Tullan, Tulapan). And it is sd to be the place where he, 'the great father-priest,' was, – where, in fact, according to a Quiche-Maya tale, he gave the first captain who set out for Guatemala-Yucatan, a present called 'Giron Gagal.' (What in christ that is, nobody knows.) One other curious thing about these chronicles, is, the 'Persian' look to so many of them. (I got on to this slant, sometime ago, when I found rewriting GATE & C, that water in Sumerian is 'a,' & in Maya, 'ha.')

But this TULE is curious in other ways (not to mention the fact that, in one people's version it is on the other side of the ocean to the east, & in another, to the west): the wildest of all, is, what you will remember, that *ultima Thule*, was the outermost reach of the world to the ancients, was, to the Greeks, Thoule, or Thyle. In the light of Waddell, I should like to know (or Berard, as well as Waddell, for that matter) if that word goes back behind the Greeks to the Phoenicians, Cretans, Sumerians.

I say this, for another reason – which goes very deep into the whole question these Maya raise (and it's treacherous ground, where all that I have seen try to walk on it, have fallen for the most dangerous Nordicism there is). But it is this evidence (you see it all around you here, and clearly not from Spanish mixture) that there was an Armenoid-Caucasian physical

46

type just as clearly as there was a Mongoloid type among the ancient Maya. (Hippolito, for ex., was telling Con and me – with considerable excitement – about a Lacandon Indian who was his & Stromsvik's guide when they were at Bonampak three yrs ago (these Lacandones are an isolated tribe in Chiapas, near the Guatemala border, who have stayed in a state of arrestment apparently equal to the period of the Maya *before* the cultivation of maize – which goes back, maybe, 3 millennia before Christ, or, into that area of time which coincides with the opening out of the Persian and Mediterranean world by the Sumerians.) Hippolito was struck by this man's whiteness, his scimitar of a nose, and the whole caucasianism of his mind and behavior.

The funny thing is, I have come on one Maya 'expert' who is pushing an argument – strangely enough – which is most close to Waddell's (tho this bird Jakeman obviously doesn't know Waddell at all). It is this. that the Itzas (who, he declares, were the priest-tribe of the Maya, the inventors of glyphs, astronomy, & the building) were the Caucasians, and can be distinguished precisely from the Mongoloids, who were the subject people, the farmers, the workers, etc. And of course his most telling argument (though he does not use it – though maybe he does: not sure yet) is that business of Quetzal-Kukul, as *white*, *bearded*, and from beyond the eastern sea.

Of course I balk at same, or at least resist, simply

because I take it, racism has to be kept at the end of a stick. Or put it this way: until we have completely cleaned ourselves of the biases of westernism, of greekism, until we have squared away at historical time in such a manner that we are able to see Sumer as a point from which *all* 'races' (speaking of them culturally, not, biologically) egressed, we do not have permission to weight the scale one way or another (for example, Jakeman, leaves, so far as I have read him, the invention of maize to the Mongoloids, as well as the arts of ceramics, weaving, and baskets! And *contra* (contra all these prejudiced Nordics, among whom I include Hooton, who has sd, from skull measurements, that it is true, there were Caucasian here), there remains China, ancient and modern China. Until the lads can verify that the Chinese, as well as the people of India, came off from the Tigris-Euphrates complex, they better lie low with their jump to conclude that only the Caucasian type was the civilizing type of man). ((As you know, this whole modern intellectual demarche, has, at its roots, a negative impulse, deeper, even, than the anti-Asia colonialism of Europe: at root, the search is, to unload, to disburden themselves, of Judaism, of Semitism.))

What excites me, is, a whole series of scholarly deductions which widen out the rear of the Maya sufficiently for me to pick up confirmations to my imaginative thesis of the sea, that is, of migration. (I had much joy this morning showing Martínez how the peoples of the Pacific made maps – I was using match

sticks to stand for those extraordinary charts of sticks
and twine by which the Polynesians & others made
the voyages from the Malay Peninsula out across that
space. And trying, in this still struggling Spanish –
'practico,' as they tell me, I still resist studying books
of same – to describe to him those huge out-riggers
the Pacific peoples used!) ...

9

thursday march 15

crazy, not to have written you. not doing a hell of a
lot: not well, either of us, or, for that matter much
of anyone around Lerma – peculiar weather, either
too hot or, the last three days a wild and beautiful
norther, the wind blowing the hell out of a new
moon. One day, the 1st, it was like any small Maine
fishing village in storm: not even the muchachas
out in the streets, every house barred, and severe, and
if a man about, wrapped (like pictures of Mexicans)
to his teeth in his cotton blanket (no such handsome
things as serapes here, just cheap cotton blankets – &
the choicest hat is a fucking chauffeur's cap!'

i can't
quite figure, what's wrong with me, but never
knew a better law than, if the body lags, it's somewhere else the lag is. Figure it's a huge shell-hole i'm
in, from recent firing. And me just lying there,
figuring, where i was hit, or, better, what bore & raise
of gun got me.

Anyhow, nothing raises me. And I waste time reading, murders (which all seem written by those filthies, newspapermen). (((A library of 'em, here, fr the wreck of a shrimper, American, beached on the farm of San Lorenzo, 10 kms down the road. Never read em before, much.)))

Went off by myself, the grey day, down the rd to sd farm, just for the motion. And by god picked myself off another ruin: right the hell on top of a little mt right the hell up over the sea! These Maya shure went for vistas ...

But it's hieroglyphs, which are the real pay-off, the inside stuff, for me. And that's not in situ, that is, you can't *see* them – why Sánchez is so very much the value, for me, here (he came to dinner Monday night, and by god if he doesn't come in with the whole set of little books published in Campeche with his drawings of same, damndest sweetest present, and, too much, as you'd say, too much ...

What wilds me, is, that here, in these things, is the intimate art (as against the mass & space of the buildings (god-stuff), and the corn-god, woman-temple, sacrifice-stone (the social purpose))

Or Jaina! Jesus, what work, there: the only trouble is, they know, and it's guarded, & for me to dig, no go: have to be an official, have to be what I was talking about, above: just one thing, in Museo, Campeche, two clay things, abt a hand's span tall, of the calix of a flower with a human being rising, right where the pistil would be! Incredible delicacy, & sureness: as in the glyphs, only, the glyphs already one stage formal, one stage set: the same glyphs, with variations, fr north to south! (What a bunch of live, working men, in this business, there were, wherever, there was a site: ex., down the road, Sunday before last, a place called Pueblo Nuevo, the site no more than 75 feet over-all, and spang, there still, a stone-glyph!) ...

Still going along on Venus, or, as they called her, *Noh ek* (the great star) or, *xux ek* (the wasp star – which sounds, this way: shoosh ek)

& the story seems to be, her attraction, beside her brightness, there for all to see, is: she's the asymmetrical one, of the Big Three, she's the one who is off the count, and does not put in regular appearance: works on a round of 584 days, but, is a real witch, in that she is two, that is, for eight months is morning star, then disappears completely for three months, to reappear as evening star for eight months, after which time she takes a dive for 14 days, to begin again, to be born, out of the eastern sea, from the balls of, her father, the sun

I like her, and like that they called her – why – the wasp, why ...

monday, mars (Or, as I figure it comes out, on the
                    Maya calendar: CEH, day AKBAL
                    (Ceh meaning the New Fire Ceremony,
                    Instituted by Kukulkan, 1159 AD or c.

... yesterday was a bitch, & beautiful: we took 7 A.M.
bus down coast, to a glyph, then set off up the road
back, walking some 8 kilometres to a place on coast
called Sihoplaya, which same beach is only equalled
by Oregon coast: we stripped, and washed each other
with the sand (not sand, but minute fragments of
shells) and crawled around that whiteness and green,
out into a submarine garden.

                                   But the sun is already
beyond taking, at midday, and of course, like mad
dogs, we get caught out: we ended, under a small
bridge over the only tidal river between here & the
next large town, Chapoton. At which place the bus
caught me in as I was born, in, that thing which is
like beginning, for me (tagged by the Annisquam), a
tidal, same! So much slugged today, too much to rise
to, in the mails, (1) Tozzer's Maya Grammar (by air
mail thru Corman) and (2) MAP of sites hereabout fr
Tulane. So I write you, to cheer me up! And for the
hell of it, let me send you a leetla thing, for the throw,
for what it is, notes, for a beginning

The fish is speech. Or see
what, cut
in stone
starts. For

when the sea breaks, watch
watch, it is the
tongue, and

he who introduces the words (the
interlocutor), the
beginner of the word, he

you will find, he
has scales, he
gives off motion as

in the sun the wind the light, the fish
moves

I I

lerma march 27

Over the house, last night, 3 A.M., the SOUTHERN
CROSS! please tell Slater that, & that, with a flash-
light, I confirmed it with, his map: tell him, the SC
here, is, at that hour, much like, & a gentler, say,
feminine counterpart to, earlier, in the west, ORION:
tell him, another thanks, for his drawings & note, on

53

the SeaHorse (which came in yesterday, along with yr other testimonial)

tell him this: that, it is quite quite true, that, here, the life of a night sky is very thick & close – and that same fact i have not seen anywhere admitted as good & sufficient reason for the Maya exploitation of same, that, in fact, in contrast to the day, which is so god-damn strong it is whited out, is, so pervasive as to make it necessary that one either blind oneself to it or hide, the night is delicious, & the sky so swift in the passage of the constellations, in the play of their colors, that it is impossible to leave

(one good & sufficient reason why there was, here, a class of men who mastered this other life is, I just bet, that, if you could choose, if you did not have to work fields, or whatever, by the light of, the sun, then, by god, you'd do what I've always sd any civilized man wld do, arrange it, that, you lived in the night not, the day!)

sure, the Mayans, too, hid from THE WASP, as they called her, that STAR: she gives you the jimmies right now, the other night, settling down in the west, and throwing such a fit of light & color, you'd swear she was going to blow right up in yr face then & there SHOOSH ECK

at which point i transfer to you how the Maya took it the other two citizens behaved:

moon is girl, living with grandfather, weaving. sun is not yet sun, is a young man full of himself, who wants this girl, & poses as great hunter, to win her first looking. to come closer he borrows the nature of hummingbird, but, while drinking honey out of the tobacco flowers near her house, grandpa pings him with a clay shot fr blowgun. moon picks sun-bird to bosom, then to room, then sun to consciousness, then sun to human shape, and business! he persuades her to elope. but g-pop gets rain to toss bolts at pair fleeing in canoe: sun converts to turtle and escapes, but moon, trying on crab shell, is not protected enough & is killed.

dragonflies collect moon's flesh & blood in 13 hollow logs. after 13 days sun uncovers logs, finds 1st 12 to contain all known noxious insects & snakes, which, released, spread all over the world. log 13 reveals moon, restored, to life

only moon has no cunt, ah. deer, however, remedies same defect, & sun & moon do it, the first persons to have such pleasure ((some passage of time))

enter sun's older brother, creating triangle of sky, for elder bro. is venus, who comes to live with sun & moon. sun begins to suspect there is something going on between moon & big star, they are so much together, by a trick he exposes them, & moon, dispirited, is sitting alone by riverwater when a vulture persuades her to go with him to the house of king vulture. Which she does, becoming his wife.

sun (the dope) seeking her, borrows skin of a small deer, hides under it, & when vultures come to eat what they think is the carcass of same, sun snatches one, gets on his back, & rides off to king vulture's house, where he recovers moon, who is somewhat reluctant to return

at which stage, for reasons of cause or not, sun & moon go up into the sky to assume their celestial duties. but sun finds there is one last thing he must do to this dame before all's right with the orb: the people on earth complain that because moon is so goddamned bright they can't sleep & it is always the same as day. so sun, to dim his dame's brightness, knocks out one of her eyes

the tale has this superior gimmick, for its ending: eclipses, sd the old ones, were nothing more nor less than fights between sun & moon, presumably because sun can't forget moon's promiscuity, though the Quiche have it that moon, anyway, is erratic, very much a liar (is constantly telling sun tales about the way the people on the earth misbehave, drink too much, etc.), and as difficult to understand as any bitch is.

I'mp tellink you, Robert, yure right, i got a horn by its tail! and fr the way it looks today (i mean precisely today, things keep shifting so as i cut away at my ignorance), that introductory glyph (of the fish) which led me in, was sign of where i am intended to go:

and i sure back off! for it is straight forward
into GLYPHS (like you probably smelled, the last few
communications). and that's one pisser of a task (&
the bitch of it is, is no way to raise dough to continue
here, any smart guy saying, such study is years, & in
lieu of any immediate addition to 'knowledge,' how
can you justify staying there, instead of here, to make
the same study?

which, of course, is cockeyed, for, it
is by being here where that life was that i pick up on
same, including glyphs, and would best continue, but
(again) who knows that but thee & who:

it is a joker,
straight: this way, that, these Maya are worth re-
membering because they were hot for the world
they lived in & hot to get it down by way of a language which is loaded to the gills of the FIRST
GLYPH with that kind of imagination which the
kerekters have a way of calling creative

yet i have yet to find *one* man among all who have
worked this street in the last century who is, himself, confident of his taste, is even possessed of that
kind of taste, or drive towards a hot world, which
is called creative power!

and the result, of course, is, that the discrepancy
between what the maya did and what these birds
are finding out about it is just another of those
gaps which confirm the old man in his shot, that,
it was not original sin, good bro. possum, which

was the fall of man, but o-riginal, in-nate, stupidity!

ex., glyphs: give you or me the 'alphabet,' just the
rudiments of the first meanings, plus a Maya dictionary and as full a knowledge as possible of tales
(such as the above), and by god if we wouldn't
walk all over them as to what the rest of the story
is! i swear (adding as long a time as possible just
being here to observe, not so much contemporary
maya (another of the wise boys' phoney smart-
nesses) but the *geography* in which the old maya
lived.

excuse me, there's no use beating you with sticks i
ought to be getting the chance to beat some others
with. and anyway, what i want to get to, with you, is,
at the nature of this *language*, of which the glyphs
are the most beautiful expression (much more beautiful, by the way, than the codices, which are late &
Mexican (pictographic, not, as were the Maya, both
ideographic & phonetic) and much more beautiful
due to the limits of stone plus the limits of language)
than the sculpture or, for that matter, the architec-
ture ...

12

lerma   wednesday   march 28

... don't let ann think, she, & los animales, marine
especially, are being left behind. for all this started fr

58

a fish (the INTRODUCTORY GLYPH), and it will come flying home, fins & all: yesterday, for example, I found further evidence (& right spang out of Sánchez's drawings) that the big boy of it all (J. Eric S. Thompson) must be wrong, when he sees the fish as a rebus of a mythological monster more like a crocodile than an actual fish (the land-bias, of the mayistas).

> Ex.: 'The fish and the Imix prefix to this god's glyph (God L, Dresden, p. 46) are probably clues to his identification (he wears fish in his headdress twice), ((Imix, sez T, is water-lily)), for both symbols are primarily those of the earth crocodile, and secondary attributes of all deities of the soil and the underworld.'

It is as underworld figure, or passenger, that T sees Quetzal-Kukan, throughout his book: that is, he is both Venus & the sun because they go down into the underworld. And so fish, water-lilies, & conch shell, because, by way of ponds, I guess, plus geologic deposits in the limestone, perhaps!, associated with his disappearance, &, reappearance! (come here, leo, fro benius!)

And you can tell Slater that Thompson hasn't even guessed at sea-horse! (He's a respectable worker, this T, but, I very much surmise he's playing with things he ain't bought the rights to. But it will take us a little time to find out!)

As a fact the beauty of Copan is, one small beauty is that it is precisely in the glyphs there (& they are the best there are, on all counts, both calendar & art) that the fish gets drawn most accurately.

I can't resist setting down one shot I made this morning, talking with Con, which, I think, opens out in several directions. I was complaining, that I have not been able to find, that any of these birds start with the simplest of a proposition when they are going on about the question, whether the glyphs were a language or not. I was saying, if they agree that the chronicles (The Books of Chilam Balam) rest on records previous to themselves (as do the codices, definitely), then, why don't they tell us – or just ask – what kind of an alphabet was it that preceded the Spanish letters in which Maya has been written since the Conquest (it is in our alphabet that the Books of Chilam Balam are written). The question answers itself: it was in hieroglyphs (the codices supplying the answer). So all that's left to answer is, was the invention of a written use contemporary, or later than, the use of same on stone? And by god if Thompson doesn't let the whole thing fall into place, without knowing it, so far as I can see now, when he tells this beautiful tale:

(preface: the codices are books, the paper was the wild fig beaten thin, and then coated with a wash of lime on which the colors and figures were 'written' – and a book was as y & x was originally

60

designed, that is, one continuous sheet of this paper (the longest known being the Codex Madrid, about 20 feet!), folded as was *y* & *x*, the text running left to right on 'pages' abt 5 inches tall & 2½ to 3 inches wide and the same left to right on the back, the book completing itself on the back of page 1: many of the pages are simply in red and black on the white lime, but in some places the details or backgrounds are in blue-green, light & dark yellow, brown, red, pink, black, all of several tones). ok.

Very destructible. Only three survived. However, sometimes codices were buried with the so-called 'priests,' or the learned men, which, still, I'd prefer to call 'em, until I know what this was they talk abt as 'religion.' anyhow.

At this point T writes: 'This information – that the codices were buried with 'em – has been confirmed by the discovery of heaps of thin flakes of lime with painting on them in tombs at Uaxactun and San Agustin Acasaguastlan. These surely represent the sizing of pages after the vegetal backings had disintegrated. A tomb at Nebaj yielded a codex in a slightly better stage of presentation.'

The point is, Uaxactun (I can't find where the other two were). But Uaxactun is the oldest, or twin-oldest, of all the cities, and was apparently not lived in after 889 A.D. (the date of its last stela).

Well, said, it doesn't seem to say much. But i smell it as important, tho, just yet, i can't demonstrate (it opens up, the fluency of, the glyphs, for me: which is what i have felt in them since that first day i saw them through Sánchez's drawings. and leads straight on in to the heart of their meaning & design as language, not, as astrological pictographs

the distinction is, that it is necessary to separate the glyphs from the use they were put to, that is, no argument, that the major use was, to record in stone the investigations by the learned of time & planets, but – because the stone has stayed, while another use – for books, painted or written with a brush – has mostly disappeared, there is no reason not to come in quite fresh from the other end, and see the whole business of glyphs as, 1st, language, and, afterward, uses of same

and it is the fact that the glyphs were the alphabet of the books that puts the whole thing back to the spoken language. Or so it seems to me, this morning.

and with that established, it would seem that the Maya language as we have had it since it got the Spanish alphabet should be, by way of its sounds, the clue to the meanings of that two-thirds of the glyphs which are still wholly unknown

I worked out, yesterday, this, as the method I'd like to follow:

the glyphs
(their design & rhythms, in addition to
what denotation the scholars have found)

the present Maya lang-uage (for its sounds & meanings, not its ortho-graphy)	*all surviving tales, re-cords, 'poems,' songs etc: the 'literature'* (Books of Chilam Balam, plus Co-dices, plus)

and that means as much Mexican Indian as Mayan
(or, for that matter, North American Indian, for you
undoubtedly tasted an old flavor in that tale of the
moon i sent you yesterday, eh?) ((I still prefer what
Sumerians incised on clay!))

But all this is too fucking bearing down to bother you
with. Let me shut up, and, instead, shoot you, quick,
other impressions which have been coming in:

(1) that these Maya were a damned nice uncertain,
uneasy, nervous, fragile bunch of humans with
eyes wide open, and jumpy, like a bird or animal, in the midst of, themselves as creatures and
the seasons & the stars – (ex., the way the sun,
moon, venus come out, in that story; and all
over the place the way they never set anything
symmetrical, even, the sun (don't know, but
just wonder if, those peoples who plug the sun
aren't always, warriors, cutthroats, like the late

63

Mexican (aztecs, or, even earlier, the chichemecs)

((another: at Copan only *one* glyph with the
head of a snake split open, and the design made
as the Alaskans did it, by the symmetry of, such,
a paper cut-out – in other words the danger,
the stereotype, of the very formalism of which
the maya were masters

on the other hand, the way, the glyphs never
got out of hand (out of media) as did the archi-
tecture & the pots, running, to naturalism, say,
the danger of the other side, the openness, the
intimate)) the way they kept the abstract alert

& (2) time: Copan D answers, for me, the whole con-
tradiction I had felt, fr that fact that Morley &
the rest keep blowing bubbles, abt, ah, the
mayah, and time-ah! shit, sd i: no people i'm
committed to could be devoted to time as these
loose-heads say they were, but i knew no answer, and, surely they did spend a hell of a lot
of time on time, surely

but the first chance i get, and can get a copy of
Copan D to send you, will, so that you can see,
that time, in their minds, was *mass & weight!*
and they even doubled the onus, making, in
Copan D, as well as generally, making the *number* of the given time unit (20, say, of 20 days)
the carrier of the burden of, the unit itself!

that is, Copan D is a date 9 baktuns (400 yrs)
                    15 katuns (20 yrs)
                    5 tuns (year of 360)
3905 yrs total   0 uninal (month of
                                20 days)
                    0 kin (day)

it is pictured thus:

man 9 carrying baktun (a huge zopalote) on his back (as the woodsmen still carry their baskets, by the band across their forehead)

man 15 wrestling with katun (same vulture, only, clawing)

man 5 somewhat pleased with himself for now carrying a dead vulture over his shoulder

etc.

well, lad, i'll quit, go for a swim, eat and shove off again for Campeche for another session with Sánchez over his drawings: we get a solid two hours in, working them over, together – and it's good, damned good ...

sunday   april 1

... What continues to hold me, is, the tremendous
levy on all objects as they present themselves to
human sense, in this glyph-world. And the proportion, the distribution of weight given same parts of
all, seems, exceptionally, distributed & accurate, that
is, that
    sun
        moon
            venus
                other constellations & zodiac
    snakes
        ticks
            vultures
    jaguar
        owl
            frog
    feathers
        peyote
            water-lily
    not to speak of
    fish
        caracol
            tortoise
    &, above all,

human eyes
    hands
        limbs (PLUS EXCEEDINGLY
                CAREFUL OBSERVA-
                TION OF ALL POS-
                SIBLE INTERVALS OF
                SAME, as well as ALL
                ABOVE (to precise di-
                mension of eclipses,
                say, & time of, same
                etc. etc.)

And the weights of same, each to the other, is, im-
maculate (as well as, full)

That is, the gate to the center was, here, as accurate
as what you & i have been (all along) talking about
- viz., man as object in field of force declaring self
as force because is force in exactly such relation &
can accomplish expression of self as force by conjecture, & displacement in a context best, now, seen as
space more than a time such;

                     which, I take it, is pre-
cise contrary to, what we have had, as 'humanism,'
with, man, out of all proportion of, relations, thus,
so mis-centered, becomes, dependent on, only, a whole
series of 'human' references which, so made, make
only anthropomorphism, and thus, make mush of,
any reality, conspicuously, his own, not to speak of,
how all other forces (ticks, water-lilies, or snails) become only descriptive objects in what used to go with

antimacassars, those, planetariums (ancestors of gold-
fish bowls) etc.

This gate got to, gone in by, 2nd stage, follows, that
is, *invention* produces narration & verse also of a contrary order (the last example of which, which comes
down to us, being, ODYSSEY

which, for my dough,
is not good enough (ditto only modern example
know, one melville), simply because humanism is
(homer) coming in, and (melville) going out

and i take
it, a Sumer poem or Maya glyph is more pertinent to
our purposes than anything else, because each of
these people & their workers had forms which un-
folded directly from content (sd content itself a disposition toward reality which understood man as
only force in field of force containing multiple other
expressions

one delightful fact, just picked up: that
all Mayan jobs (sez Tatiana Proskouriakoff) are built
around *a single human figure*, in all reliefs, etc.

which is, of course, that ego which you, me, Mayan
X were (are), he who is interested enough to, seeing
it all, get something down

What has to be battered down, completely, is, that
this has anything to do with stage of development.
Au contraire. The capacity for (1) the observation &
(2) the invention has no more to do with brick or

68

no wheels or metal or stone than you and i are different from, sd peoples: we are like. Therefore, there is no 'history.' (I still keep going back to, the notion, this is (we are) merely, the *second time* (that's as much history as I'll permit in, which ain't history at all: seems so, only, because we have been all dragooned into a notion that, what came between was, better. Which is eatable shit, for the likes of those who like, same.

Animation of what presents itself, fr the thing on outwards: rock as vessel, vessel as tale, creating, men & women, because narrator and/or poet happen to be man or woman, thus, human figure as part of universe of things

(Other things, of same, the provocations, say:

the *eye*, in Mayan (other Indian as well) & Sumerian fixes (jesus, in these glyphs, how, or stones, how, with *any* kind of device, the eye takes up life (contra Greek, Rome, even, Byzantine): ex., Museo, Campeche, a wonderful little 'monster' with eyes made so

and the hands (fingers):

this is peculiarly brilliant at
Copan (as I sd), where, if any dancer now living had
sense, he'd be, finding out, how, to exploit this part
of his, instrument

> not to speak of how the face is, the
> other dominant glyph in addition to
> the abstracts of all other natural
> forms, is, the human or animal
> *heads* ...

14

friday april 6 (It's 3 P.M., at which hour I have just
had breakfast, which may be a gauge, the 15 hrs, of
the toll of woods & ruins: two days, & a day of pre-
paration for same – Con not able to go along, so,
alone, whatever better than 200 kilometers is, away
fr here. And the craziest of it, being, put up, the night
before last in a jail! At Santa Elena, the very town, it
turned out afterwards, where Stephens based himself
100 yrs agone, when he hit same sites:

Uxmal & Kabah   (((found out, it's tick poisoning,
                    which, I've had: you shld not
                    be me, this morning, with my
                    trunk wholly raised in sores,
                    plus, fr the jail water, tourista,
                    viz, GIs: up at 6 this morn-
                    ing))) ...

15

.. Bushed, hoy. And precisely the verb. For, the bush, of Jaina, leaves me so. Jesus, what a job these lands are, in the sun! Impossible, the way, the sun drags you down – in one half hr it is eating you, its clawing having pulled you off yr pins. Wicked. I tried, for awhile, to scratch away at the walls of the graves (one leaps in to holes which are exactly like the stage holes into which Hamlet leaps). But there, with what breeze there is coming fr the sea (and there was good breeze yesterday) cut off, one can't take more than 5 minutes! I'm telling you, lad, one thing is hugely proved: one can't touch this Yucatan (or I'd gather, any place of these Maya) without full expeditionary equipment. Which, of course, means, institutions. Ergo, mal.

Any one place requires, instantly, two to three days: that is, all one can do the first day, is to get there. For by that time the sun is too far up to do anything but sleep in some place out of the sun. So that evening, and the next morning, early, are the only work times. Which means, almost, the 3rd day, for return. All of which is too expensive for the likes of one sole adventurer as me!

We got away at 5 A.M., the lad, who was to sail us, having, I guess, spent too long at the baile the night before, for, tho we were up before 4, the two of us, he didn't show until almost five.

The run was lovely: 4 hrs, with a strong following wind, so strong the cayuco, in the hour before the sun came, was heeled over so, her gunwale was taking water! And by god if Con wasn't way the hell out in front of me, taking it! And it her first time in a fisherman! Tho I shld say, she knows sailing boats, I, never, previously, having been under sail except in schooners. Wonderful rich sea. And after, with the wind losing that first freshness, under double sail, going like hell across the gulf, straight run, almost due north fr here: a fine lad, 24, 10 yrs fisherman, without grace, but handling his boat confidently.

Hit Jaina abt 9:30, left at 3:00. So it was the meanest part of the day that we had to work. Result: no chance to take away – to find any of the great clay with which the whole 'island' is soaked: it is, it, whole length & width (approximately a circle, diameter abt half a mile), a cemetery: in fact, the water has intruded on the land on the seaward side considerably, and in the waters offshore one can spot the tell-tale scattering of pieces of pots (literally, as the lady sd, like, rose-petals, literally, color and all – a tho the Maya brought boatloads and threw handful as some sort of a gesture of farewell or protection to those, they buried there).

Craziest damn thing ever, this place: nothing on it otherwise but two sets of double small pyramids at either end of the 'island': one to seaward, one toward the land (now, of course, just rounded hills). And not even raisings where the graves are, as, say, like 'ours'! Just a flat island, abt like (with the two raised ends looking, fr seaward, as dunes) coming on the coast, there, abt Ipswich, say! Only difference, that, the shore is, mangrove.

But here's the punch-line: a damned attractive place, as place, so much so it occurred to both C & me, was it the reason the Maya (from wherever they came to this jut of the land driving out into the sea just here, to bury their, dead) did so come here, choose, this place?

Must find out more. There've been 3 expeditions to dig same, and, the 1st I imagine, found a glyph stone here with the date 652 A.D. Which is one of the earliest dates known north of Guatemala. And long before the building of the major cities of the north. Know no bibliography on the place, only, one lousy book Pavon & a guy named Pina Chan did, on the graves, 3 yrs ago. (Figure on this, as on so many things, I shall have to find out by reading reports in the Instituto Nacional in Mex City, where, all mss of expeditions are collected.)

I'd guess one thing: if we had gone up there when we first came, I'm sure I'd have wanted to promote us a singleteam expeditionary force to live there awhile, and dig. For it has the damndest charm, the place. And one roofless building at the landing (dating back to Spanish 18th century) in which to live with an ancient well there in which the loveliest doves (very small, no more than five inches overall) hide.

I slept, awhile, on the return, folded in under the thwarts, out of the sun which had spent me, and fitting the bottom just like one of its knees: it was a throwback, for me, to the way it was sleeping, in a schooner's peak, with the water's sounds coming in through the wood of the planks ...

One can buy one of these cayucos, complete with double sails, for 250 bucks! And the rest of the time back Con and I played with the notion of borrowing some such dough to buy same and to return to the States so! (Turned out it would take two months, the lad sd, just to get, by the coast, to Vera Cruz!) But what an idea, eh? And fine, while it lasted!

Well. Just to keep you, in. Am weak like sick, and so no words, hoy. But damned happy to have been there: if you had seen any of these small clay figures they buried clutched in the hands of their dead, you'd know why. They are intimate, close human things, these – what the dopes call – 'anthropomorphic' figurines. Jesus. Or 'zoomorphic'! And two (here in the Museum) are those I guess I must have men-

tioned to you: of the calyx of clay with little human
sitting where the pistil might be?

And no telling what else is there, the place has no
been really dug at all: a couple of halfhearte
'trenchings' of the pair of pyramids. And spotted ex
humations of, the graves (the graves go right to th
mangrove edge! must have been dug right in sal
water!

        what bend of mind motivated thi
place? from how far did the people come who cam
here to bury? how did they come, by sea? for th
the 'island' is only more of the land furruled by
breakings in of, water, there is nothing inside to in
dicate any human settlements for great distance
damned funny, the whole, business (and, so far as
know, no other similar example anywhere among th
Maya, tho, I should have liked very much to hav
gone around to the East coast & seen Isla Mujere
Cozumel, and Tulum, over there, where, the May
were coastal and thick . . . .

16

sun apr 29 51

... for RC :

76

	(architecture)	(ceramica)	(date)
EARLY DEVELOP-	PRE-MASONRY	MAMOM ?	
MENTAL			(1000 yrs) ?
LATE DEVELOP-	PRE-VAULT	CHICANEL ?	
MENTAL			ditto-278 A.D.

((in EARLY, no buildings, much flint, & pottery
    figurines; in LATE, 1st formal plaza idea,
    but, only at very end, truncated pyramids
    with wood superstructures), & no pot. figs.))

EARLY CLASSIC	VAULT I	TZAKOL
		278-593 A.D.

(1) glyphs (2) stone superstructs. (3) burials, in
    crypts, instead of just turned up, ground (4)
    many-colors, on pots (5) jade

LATE CLASSIC	VAULT II	TEPEXU
		593-889 plus

(meaning, the climax of,   wider windows, bigger
building) stone for veneer, rooms
the carefully cut pieces we
find at our cuyo thin walls,

abandonment of site, even tho site still top shape!

for Ann:

as against the agronomy explanations of, the abandonment of, the southern cities, AVKidder argues, excellently, that it won't hold (either (1) that they maized-out, the soil, or (2) that they cut off so many zapote trees, they got erosion, & silted up their lakes into malaria swamps), simply because such sites as Quirigua (on the river Montagua, which, floods like the Nile, offsetting either of above explanations, obviously) and the Usumacinta sites (river, again : Piedras Negras, Palenque) *were also deserted when*, the other, inlands, were! Copan, likewise! which sits, even today, ready, for, occupancy

for SB:

Uaxactun answers, on water: had exact reservoirs, very much the same as, ours ((see Ricketson & Ricketson, 1937, Carnegie Pub. 477, pp. 9-11; & A. Ledyard Smith, 1950, same, No. 588, pp. 61, 84))

natural clay removed to depth of (in one case, the smaller of two, 7½ feet at center) and graded to surrounding ground level

the bottom had then been covered with 3 inch deposit of sand on which was laid a pavement of large stone slabs which, in turn, were covered by a 7 inch layer of sand (Late Classic)

he larger, is an almost circular one, about 100 feet in
iameter and better than 16 feet deep! With a dam of
atural ravine to feed in water on that side, and, –
y god, on the other – on the side towards the cause-
vay joining the two elements of the city which the
ros. call Group A and Group B, if, by god, these lads
adn't cut a sluice in the parapet of the causeway so
hat, all drainage from all inclined city squares
owed, during the rainy season – the agua lluvia one
ears these present people talking abt like they talk
bt the weather these dry days (they have to pay 30
entavos a water vase for it, just abt now, fr., big
hots with, exactly the same inclined run-offs, here-
bouts, now, individually owned, and charged for,
ontra, then, eh?) – a SPILLWAY, no less, constructed
by the evidence of the pot fragments in the fill, just
bove, the bedrock) Early Classic, that is, between
oo and 600 A.D.

k

17

unday   july 1

.. the thing on my mind today is, a feeling, that this
vould be a damned good place to be the hell out of
he mess which I expect to grow worse up there
o the north, as well as generally in Europe and Asia,
he next few years …

The point is, a double one: (1) that I have, somehow
to work out an economic 'modo' to pay me while
write verse, anywhere, and (2) that a buck, here
works at least three times as hard. And if this India
stuff can be made to do it, I don't think of a bette
jointure. For their nouns, undone, are my nouns.

Ex: Alfonso

(Mariano's 7 yr old brother) came up with thi
yesterday. His brother-in-law is a farmer, back i
the hills. And that toc bird – the one I may hav
described to you, that picks its own tail away t
beautify itself (or so Stromsvik taught me), leav
ing the end only, which is a peacock's eye
troubles this poor farmer, troubles him so, h
stones them because, says he, can't look into th
mirror of that tail, it frightens him, so he has t
smash it!

Which goes right to the heart of th
matter. For that damned bird just does use i
tail as though it were a mirror, switching
around like proud lady does her own – for a
miration!

What would lay you in the aisles, is a Sunda
(today), to see these fishermen (7–13), after six day
in cayucos with their pas or older brothers, real liv
cayucos on real live gulf with god-damned dangerou
northers coming off the American continent, or, th
season, chubascos loaded with rain from the ea
(from the trades, and their collision with this thum
of land, the peninsula), running or swimming up an

own the beach here outside me sailing their own-made toy cayucos! Damndest mix-up ever. The same ads you'd have seen last night, with white shirts buttoned up in that queer old-fashioned shallow collar, taking the night air with their fellow fishermen, their elders, on the plaza – doing everything the others do of a Saturday night except get drunk on the bad rum and good beer!

There is this lad, 9, who, for the past two years, has, as the oldest in his family, his father dead, somehow managed to bring in 6 pesos a day. And now fishes, probably taking 10, say, a day – and thus the principal support now, that he is a fisherman. Or is he 11, and has been doing it since 9? Maybe that's it. But what the hell – the scale is crazy, however you look at it.

And by god none of them get enough to eat, even so. And I do not mean by gorging American comparisons. By minimums. 4 eggs, for example, for an omelet for a family of 7! (This is the hardest part of it here, the business, of what we buy, as against them, to maintain our own habits – which, despite my size, are nothing compared to my fellow cits. It bothers Con so much she will hand over the money to me to keep from giving it away! Or will buy less pork than she wants, or less oranges, from the eyes which watch her at the store!

There is one guy, Chica, whom we do not
know enough to peg. He seems to be employed
by the town, for odd jobs. But he is poor,
whether from laziness, as Chappy says, or
from the disabilities of scarlet fever (is it?) or
malaria, as others say. In any case, he is a
shrewd beggar, and has a nose to hang at the
door of the store just when Con has to cash
a 50 peso bill! The other day, she just couldn't
do it, and though she had shown the bill to
the store people, she asked, in the end, seeing
Chica, to charge what she had bought! But
fortunately, the time he hit me, hard, I gave
in. I looked out the window (some distance
from the door at which he had knocked) and
sure enough, there was, at the door, a woman
who he sd was his wife, and she did have, as
I could see from the lump in her rebozo, what
he said was their baby, who was sick, he sd,
and would I give him 5 pesos to take it to a
doctor. Thank God. For though it did not save
the thing's life, it was that sick, he did have
the chance to have it get the injections which
they all believe, around here, is what solves
all troubles!

Even to our medicines, we have
these people 'conquered,' god help them.

It's just the last remnant of the older life – that life
which had been man's way all that time until our
generation – that gives this place still its resonance

This morning, it was too much, to wake to the sort of noises which they make here the day they don't work, and set out for chicharrons (pork scraps) which are the day's delicacy. Or last night to go off for ice, and be confronted, on the main street, with a horse racing toward me in the street-light dark, and not being able to figure out what the hell is the light thing riding it, until, they are almost on me, and I have to squeeze up against the building, by this time knowing, and nervous, they'll shy, for it's a stallion mounting her, and going like hell the two of them, scaring the old ladies in their rockers out on the sidewalk, and all the guys at the square roaring with laughter at this invasion from the country!

Con figures, the animals, can't any more resist Saturday night in town – paseo, Senor y Senora, pasanado? – than any of us can. Every Saturday night – and no other night, by god, if three goats don't come in and chew their way through it all! And precisely ma, pa, and little goat! Exactly like a Maya family in, from the farms, back of Quila!

It's crazy. And to feel the crash of the American noises blot out these other older things! The buses and trucks and convertibles, the Birdseye freezing plant's generators, and the planes! It's – here – being on the divide, precisely at watershed.

And it has a personal wallop. For it puts me almost exactly where things were, in the States, when I was

etc. Crazy, to feel that same bouncing, from yourself
Damned refreshing.

Don't but see but what we are the legitimate bearer
of value, simply because, we have known it, both
ways, the first, to so know what men can do. To cu
in, right there, where what was can be coolly known
and what is, can be separated from, hope: what
spot! Like it, myself, and think we damn well hav
the advantage of our elders – and better use same
instead, as I mostly observe, fall back (even Ez, th
greatest) or fall on our face, as most. (Again, DHI
seems the only one who, didn't mug either, whc
stood there, getting it, as his own).

Well, lad, from Lerma then, no goodbye, but just, i
passing, the word. The 'Lucero di Alba' is now re
ported for tomorrow, which means we ought to b
off about Thursday, the 5th, is it, getting us to Pensa
cola the 8th – or a day or so later, I'd guess, know
ing the stevedores in this hyar port. So we'll be ;
couple of days late arriving at North Carolina, nc
that it matters. Except that I shall be hungry for som
mail from you. Keep it piling up, please. I should lik
to make the switch without breaking stride, but tha
surely, is a fool's dream ...

*　　*　　*

'The scientific bias taken by our civilization has ... given to History and Archeology a role, valuable and respectable, of course, but not inspired.'
— Edward Hyams,
Soil & Civilization
(Thames & Hudson, 1952)

(1) in such a category:

J. Eric S. Thompson, *Mayan Hieroglyphic Writing: Intro-duction*
(Carnegie Institution, 1950)

THE MAYA AND THEIR NEIGHBORS, essays in honor of Alfred Tozzer (D. Appleton-Century, 1940), especially Oli-ver G. Ricketson Jr.'s 'Outline of Basic Physical Factors Affect-ing Middle America' also Earn-est Hooton's debunking of sac-rifice by analysis of skeletons from the Cenote at Chichen Itza

A. V. KIDDER's hypothesis of civil war as explanation of the 'deserted cities,' in his

introduction of the Carnegie
publication of the work of the
Smiths at Uaxactun & – merely
to have the glyphs to look at,
and in lieu of any existing publication of the drawings from the
glyphs by Hippolito Sánchez –
Morley's *The Inscriptions at
Copan*, and *The Inscriptions of
Peten* (Carnegie Institution,
1920, 1937-38)

The climax still, of all such work is Bul-
letin No. 28 of the Bureau of American
Ethnology, 24 papers on 'Mexican and
Central American Antiquities' by Seler,
Forstemann, Schellhas, Sapper and Diesel-
dorff, edited by Bowditch (Washington,
Government Printing Office, 1904)

(2) not so respectable,
   but stabs at value,
   on the language question:

the long work of William E.
Gates, from 1910 to 1940, published by the Maya Society, Bal-
timore, and including his outline dictionary of Maya glyphs,
1931;

& – though here I am as
doubting as Thompson is chol-

eric – B. L. Whorf's four papers on Maya, among his many on other languages, and on language itself.

(*Note*: how questionable Whorf's work is may be judged by the free ride it is just now getting from those sinister rightists, the semantic people, who come out of that 'human engineering' one, Non-A Korzybski)

3) Neither Archaeology
nor History, but
the only intimate
and active experience
of the Maya yet
in print:

JOHN L. STEPHENS, two books, *Incidents of Travel in Central America, Chiapas, and Yucatan* (N. Y., 1841), and *Incidents of Travel in Yucatan* (N. Y., 1843), with Frank Catherwood's drawings in each, of *ruinas*, and of the stelae, for checking against Sánchez. (Prescott and Parkman are a triad: Stephens is the unacknowledged third.)

Also – a guess on my part –
the scattered work, and unpub
lished manuscripts, of ROBER
BARLOW, dead, by his own
hand, January, 1951

II

'This "poet's technique" ha
rarely been applied to the stud
of the past and perhaps neve
to the study of the remot
past.'

                              – Hyams, op. ci
(the preceding sentence to pr
vious quote from him)

D. H. Lawrence did. And Melville, before him:
                    ex., Lawrence, preface, FANTA
                    SIA OF THE UNCONSCIOUS
                    where he imagines states o
                    being & geography divers fro
                    the modern
Nor is it a 'technique.' It is disposition, to reality. An
can be precisely known, as is.

But the matter here is to isolate the works of thes
two men as the only ones who have so 'applied,' 't
the study of,' since Herodotus ('History' came int
being with Herodotus's exact contemporary, Thucy

dides), and to go on to discriminate other works which, because they are of the past as it is not merely History or Archaeology, enable one to give the Maya the present they once were, and are:

> Brooks Adams, *The New Empire* (N. Y., 1902, with maps), for the scope of its trade-and-money story, even if eventually any of his work is boring from the capitulation in him to the machine as sufficient analogy for all process

> Leo Frobenius' books on Africa, Rock Paintings, and Paideuma, despite questions; his 'Childhood of Man,' one of his earliest, is still, so far as I know, the only one translated into English.

> Jane Harrison, anything of hers, notably (for me) *PROLEGOMENA to the Study of Greek Religion*

> Pausanias's *Description of Greece*, more valuable than Plutarch, his immediate predecessor, c. 100 A.D., because of

its careful localism, and taking
what is said as how to find out
for oneself

Ezra Pound, *Guide to Kulchur*,
just because it razzledazzles
History. And any Learning. But
its loss is exactly that. Plus the
poet's admitted insistence he
will stay inside the Western
Box, Gemisto, 1429 A.D., up

Carl O. Sauer, 'Environment
and Culture in the Deglaci-
ation,' American Philosophical
Society, 1947, the single gate to
the remote past; see also his
'American Agricultural Origins:
A Consideration of Nature and
Culture,' in Essays in Anthro-
pology in Honor of Alfred
Kroeber (Berkeley, 1936)

(Addendum, Attic, Annex, Any
 hidden place:

for those who have the wit to tell the Unconscious
when they see one, or for the likes of me, who was
raised on the American Weekly, there are at least two
men I want to mention (not to speak of Ignatius Don-

ɪelly on Atlantis, Churchward on Mu – or, for that
ɪnatter, Rider Haggard!):

ɪhe Frenchman, Victor Berard, Mediterranean explorer
ɪvho wrote several books to show that the *Odyssey*
ɪwas a rewrite from a Semitic original; and a Scot,
ᷛ. A. Waddell, also an explorer, of Tibet, who was
ɪsure that the Sumerians or the Hittites or the Trojans
ɪfounded the British Hempire, and that Menes the
ɪEgyptian was Minos the Cretan and ended up dead,
ɪfrom the bite of a wasp, in Ireland, at Knock-Many,
ɪthe 'Hill of Many,' in County Tyrone.

But no one but
ɪan herodotean may fool around with such fraudu-
ɪlence & fantasy practiced on document (instead of on
ɪthe galaxies), no matter how much such stories are,
ɪto my taking, the body of narrative which has inter-
ɪvened between the great time of fiction & drama (the
ɪCity-time) and the present (which is no time for fan-
ɪtasy, drama – or City).

The trouble is, it is very diffi-
ɪcult, to be both a poet and, an historian.

October, 1953

SELECTED BIBLIOGRAPHY

The principal works of Charles Olson, with the dates of
their first appearance

CALL ME ISHMAEL
   (Reynal & Hitchcock, New York, 1947)

LETTER FOR MELVILLE
   (Black Mountain College, N. Carolina, 1951)

MAYAN LETTERS
   (Divers, Mallorca, 1953)

THE MAXIMUS POEMS 1–10
   (Jargon Press, Highlands, N. Carolina, 1953)

PROJECTIVE VERSE
   (Totem Press, New York, 1959)

THE DISTANCES
   (Grove Press, New York, 1960)

THE MAXIMUS POEMS
   (Jargon/Corinth Books, New York, 1960)

THE HUMAN UNIVERSE
   (Auerhahn Society, San Francisco, 1965)

THE AUTHOR

Charles Olson was born in 1910 at Worcester, Massachusetts and, as he likes to put it, 'uneducated' at Wesleyan, Yale, and Harvard Universities. After teaching at Clark and at Harvard, he was instructor and Rector at the famous Black Mountain College, North Carolina, from 1951 to 1956. Since then, Olson has received Guggenheim Fellowships to do research in the Maya area of Mesoamerica and a Wenner-Gren Foundation grant to study Maya hieroglyphics (1952). In recent years he has been living in Gloucester and writing the Maximus Poems and has taught at the University of Buffalo in New York State. Today he is one of the leading figures in the Pound–Williams lineage which includes Zukofsky, Oppen, Duncan, Creeley, and Snyder.

CAPE EDITIONS